MW00812686

ARIBERT MUNZNER
TEACHER, COLLEAGUE, ARTIST

MINNEAPOLIS COLLEGE OF ART AND DESIGN

2000

For Ari with best wishes   *Roman 98*

Ari Munzner, 1998.
Digital Photograph: MCAD Professor Emeritus, Roman Verostko.
Iris print on Arches paper.

Published by the Minneapolis College of Art and Design
2501 Stevens Avenue, Minneapolis, Minnesota 55404
612/874-3700   www.mcad.edu

MCAD Emeritus Series: Volume One
Copyright 2000 Minneapolis College of Art and Design
All rights reserved

ISBN cloth 0-9611672-2-X
First Edition

No part of this book may be used or reproduced
without express permission from the publisher,
except in the context of reviews.

Printed and bound in the U.S.A.

The page and grid structure of this book is based
on the proportions of Ari's *Micro Drawings*, 2.5" x 2".
Cover art: calligraphy from *Genesis Artist's Statement*,
1999; photograph by Roman Verostko, 1998.

The fonts used in this book are Weiss and Frutiger.
Weiss was designed in 1926 by Rudolph Weiss.
Based on classic Roman faces, the character of Weiss
emanates its origins in humanist Renaissance tradition.
Frutiger, designed in 1968 by Adrian Frutiger, is a
highly legible sans serif, originally intended as the
"house font" for the de Gaulle Airport.

Editor: Lynn Golberstein
Design: Pamela Arnold

The Minneapolis College of Art and Design (MCAD)
is an accredited member of the National Association
of Schools of Art and Design.

*Founded in 1886, the Minneapolis College of Art and Design is
an independent, accredited institution offering a four-year curriculum
integrating the Liberal Arts into 14 professional B.F.A. degree majors
in Fine Arts, Media Arts and Design; a four-year BS degree program
in Visualization; a two-year M.F.A. degree program in Visual
Studies; a one-year Post Baccalaureate certificate program as well as
educational opportunities for the general public through Continuing
Studies, distance learning and exhibition programs. All MCAD
programs challenge students to progress to the highest levels of artistic
expression and intellectual investigation.*

The drawings and paintings reveal the universality of art and science
through the metaphor of microcosm and macrocosm.

Aribert Munzner, 1999

"When I was working on the Micro drawings, someone said to me, 'You know, you really ought to paint larger. I mean, you're working with Genesis.' And then I said, 'Oh yeah? Larger than the studio? You mean larger than the city? Larger than the planet? Larger than the galaxy?' But I said to myself, 'Okay, so how small can I get?' And I got smaller and smaller and smaller."

— Ari Munzner, excerpted from a conversation about art, July 12th, 1999

Ari in front of *Genesis 65-9*, 3M Scanamural Color Experiment, 1979.
132" x 108": acrylic on canvas.
Photo: Shirley Luke Schnell, MCAD B.F.A. Painting, 1958.

Selected Collections

Walker Art Center, Drawing Collection, Minneapolis, Minnesota

Tweed Museum, Duluth, Minnesota

Grey Art Center, New York University, New York

Zhejiang Academy of Art, Hangzhou, China

Archer Daniels Midland Company

Lutheran Brotherhood Collection, Minneapolis, Minnesota

Maslon, Edelman, Borman & Brand, Minneapolis, Minnesota

Liberty State Bank, Saint Paul, Minnesota

Hennepin Avenue United Methodist Church, Minneapolis, Minnesota

Dolly Fiterman, Minneapolis, Minnesota

Bruce Dayton, Wayzata, Minnesota

Visiting Artist

Saint Cloud State University, 1995

North Carolina School of the Arts: 1978,1982

Kansas City Art Institute, 1979

University of Minnesota, Duluth: 1974, 1976

Yale Summer School of Art, 1974

University of New Orleans: 1972-73

Nova Scotia College of Art and Design, 1970

Experimental Grants

3M Computer Graphic BFA Paint System, 1984

3M SCANAMURAL Paint System:1979, 1982, 1984

Industrial Photo-Offset Color Lithography, 1977

Photomicroscopy with Dr. Roman Vishniac, New York City, 1971

Atlanta College of Art

College Art Association

Mid-America College Art Association

National Association of Schools of Art and Design

Alliance of Independent Colleges of Art

Electronic Vision II, Contemporary Art Center, New Orleans, Louisiana

Simulations/Dissimulations, The School of the Art Institute of Chicago

Foundation Studies Curriculum, University of Illinois, Champaign/Urbana

CHRONOLOGY

Born: Mannheim, Germany 1930

Baghdad, Iraq 1937

New York City 1939

Alton, New York 1941-1948

Syracuse University, B.F.A. 1953

Cranbrook Academy of Art, M.F.A. 1955

Minneapolis College of Art and Design, Professor 1955-1993

Minneapolis College of Art and Design, M.F.A. (Honorary)1988

Minneapolis College of Art and Design, Professor Emeritus 1994

GALLERY AFFILIATION

Dolly Fiterman Fine Arts, Minneapolis, Minnesota

Dolly Fiterman Fine Arts Gallery, *(Group)*
Minneapolis, Minnesota: 1993, 1994, 1995, 1996, 1997, 1998

Dolly Fiterman Fine Arts Gallery, *(Individual) Minneapolis, Minnesota: 1978, 1982, 1984, 1998-9*

Intermedia Arts Gallery, *(Group) Minneapolis, Minnesota: 1996, 1997, 1998*

DIDEROT *(Group) with Erika Suderburg, Southern Exposure Gallery, San Francisco, California, 1994*

FISEA–Fourth International Symposium on Electronic Art, *(Invitational)*
Minneapolis College of Art and Design, 1993

CRASH, *(ComputeR-AssiSted Hardcopy) (Invitational)*
Wright Museum of Art, Beloit, Wisconsin, 1988

Simulations/Dissimulations, *(Invitational) The School of the Art Institute of Chicago, 1987*

The Drawing Show, *(Invitational) Nash Gallery,*
University of Minnesota, Minneapolis, Minnesota, 1987

Intermedia Arts Gallery, *(Individual) Minneapolis, Minnesota, 1987*

Digital Perspectives-85, Minnesota *SIGGRAPH/NCGA Group Traveling Exhibition, 1985-86*

Electronic Visions II, *(Invitational) Contemporary Arts Center, New Orleans, Louisiana, 1985*

Developing the Critical Eye, *(Invitational) JCC, Minneapolis, Minnesota, 1985*

Allvision, with Woody/Steina Vasulka, *(Invitational) Science Museum of Minnesota, 1984*

Minnesota SIGGRAPH Competition, 3M *UCV, Minneapolis, Minnesota,1984*

Architechtonics II, *(Invitational) New Acquisitions Gallery, Syracuse, New York, 1984*

Computer Graphics, *(Invitational) MCAD, Minneapolis, Minnesota, 1982*

New Acquisitions Gallery, *(Individual) Syracuse, New York, 1982*

North Carolina School of Arts, *(Individual) Winston Salem, North Carolina: 1978,1982*

Drawing Exhibition, *(Invitational) Swain School of Design, New Bedford, Massachusetts, 1981*

Drawing Exhibition, *(Invitational) Webster College, St.Louis, Missouri, 1981*

Kansas City Art Institute, *Foundation Division Gallery, (Individual) Kansas City, Missouri, 1979*

Maharishi International University Gallery, *(Invitational) Fairfield , Iowa, 1979*

St. Catherine College Gallery *(Two-person Exhibition)* *St. Paul, Minnesota, 1977*

Retrospective, Tweed Museum, *Duluth, Minnesota, 1975*

Drawings:10 Minnesota Artists, *(Invitational) Walker Art Center, Minneapolis, Minnesota, 1971*

Walker Art Center, *(Individual) Minneapolis, Minnesota, 1971*

Northrop Gallery, *University of Minnesota, (Individual) Minneapolis, Minnesota, 1969*

Gilman Gallery, *(Individual) Chicago, Illinois 1968,*

Traveling Exhibition, *(Invitational) The Mead Corporation: 1965-66*

Drawing in Minnesota,1965 *(Invitational) Walker Art Center, Minneapolis, Minnesota, 1965*

The Little Gallery, Minneapolis Institute of Arts *(Individual) Minneapolis, Minnesota, 1965*

The Art of Two Cities, *(Invitational Traveling Exhibition) Minneapolis/Kansas City: 1965-66*

The Mulvane Art Center, *Washburn University (Group) Topeka Kansas, 1965*

National Society of Painters in Casein, *(Group) New York City, New York: 1961, 1963, 1966*

Sioux City Art Center, *(Group) Sioux City, Iowa, 1963*

Joslyn Art Museum, *(Group) Omaha, Nebraska, 1963*

Walker Art Center, *(Group) Minneapolis, Minnesota: 1960, 1961, 1962, 1965*

The Minneapolis Institute of Arts *(Group) Minneapolis, Minnesota: 1955, 1956, 1961, 1963*

Cranbrook Academy of Art, *(Invitational Traveling Exhibition) Bloomfield Hills, Michigan: 1955-6*

Contemporary Arts Gallery, *(Group) New York City, New York,1954*

City Center Gallery, *(Group) New York City, New York, 1954*

Munson-Williams-Proctor Institute, *(Group) Utica , New York,1954*

Rochester Memorial Art Gallery, *(Group) Rochester, New York: 1953, 1958*

Syracuse Museum, *(Group) Syracuse, New York: 1952, 1953*

On July 12, 1999, a small group of colleagues and former students gathered at the studio of Aribert Munzner for an informal dinner party. Our intent was to tape the dialogue and to incorporate it into the book, thereby infusing these pages with some of the spirit of this exemplary teacher and man. The conversation that follows is from that evening; this segment provides a glimpse into the world of Ari, a unique and passionate man who has become a legend in his own time.

Among the participants were DAVID NYE BROWN, PROFESSOR EMERITUS OF LIBERAL ARTS, and a dear friend to Ari and to MCAD; graduate mentees of Ari, Lynn Golberstein, M.F.A. '96 and Mark Piatkowski M.F.A. '99; Derek Haglund B.F.A. '99; and several MCAD faculty and staff members. The conversation opens with Ari's response to the question of how he came to teach at MCAD.

— Lynn Golberstein, Editor

The snapshots, that accompany this dialogue, were taken by Derek Haglund, MCAD B.F.A. 1999. Professor David Nye Brown is pictured here, engaged in characteristic dialogue with Ari.

(left) Ari Munzner, in his studio, 1998. Photo by Sean Smuda, *City Pages*.

Ari There I was at Cranbrook, it was 1955, I had just written my M.F.A. thesis. I was never going to be a teacher, I was going to go back to New York and paint. And then, Wilhemus B. Bryan, the Director of the Minneapolis School of Art, came to Cranbrook and said to my teacher, Zoltan Sepeshy, "Look, someone is leaving the MSA, What do you have here?"

So, we had a little discussion on the lawn at Cranbrook, and I showed Bryan my M.F.A. thesis. It was a three-page thesis which read, "Art Cannot be Taught." And Bryan read it and said, "So, art can't be taught? Is that right?" And then he said, "Hmmm...okay. Wanna join us?" So, the next thing I knew, I was in Minneapolis. At that time, we were a very tiny little school, the Minneapolis School of Art, inside the Morrison Building. And what was wonderful was that it was just the beginning of having a school of art that included the ideas, the humanities—philosophy, history, literature—everything.

Among those three pages of my thesis, I said only three things : that the teacher is there as a guide, as a coach, to help the person evolve in their own way, not the teacher's way; that you can introduce materials, techniques, resources, and information at the appropriate time, but the appropriate time of the student, not the teacher; and that the process of art is the process, and not the art. And that basically is the thesis and the title, "Art Cannot be Taught." Ever since then, that's what I've been doing: non-teaching and coaching whether I'm teaching a visual studies class, a basic studies class, art criticism with David, interdisciplinary studies, painting or drawing.

David   In 1958, when I came, Ari had already been here for three years. The college was in a ferment, partly because of Ari and partly because Wilhemus Bryan, who believed in the liberating consequences of the processes of studio art, had a great capacity for getting moneys from large corporations.

Ari and I soon became involved in team-teaching where Ari represented the studio and I represented the liberal arts. So I know a good deal about the history of Ari's development as an artist, and I must say, that I would rather talk about Ari's art than almost anything else in the world! His art is so thoughtful. It has to do with such profound concepts and issues that are perennial and provocative. As a student of philosophy, as well as of art, art history, and art criticism, I found that most, if not all, of the major issues or concepts are met in his work.

Genesis is, of course, the enduring theme. For me, there's another kind of analogy between the creative process, as Ari himself sees it and as I see it, and creative processes in the world—both on the macrocosmic level and the microscopic level, and on the external world level and the inner world level. One of the major insights that Ari brings to both education and to art is that there cannot be any stretching or proposing or wishing or wanting. As soon as you have a preconceived goal in mind, you are already inhibited. You are already blocked. So his procedure, his process, his method of painting, exemplifies this point of view. His small strokes are a way of setting up matrixes in which patterns emerge—none of it is preconceived. And this freedom—from purpose or intention—is the condition, the necessary condition, prerequisite for something to emerge. If one is trying to press or push, then it's not likely to happen.

ARIBERT MUNZNER
TEACHER, COLLEAGUE, ARTIST

There is also a correspondence between the painter and the painting. Every minute, with these small strokes, Ari is giving himself a chance to find out what the painting wants, or is, as well as what he is or who he is at that moment. And it's a process because there is no pushing. And that is a difficult place to be. To be in the process, to be attending to the process, to be trusting that as long as one is respecting the process, the product takes care of itself. The outcome is inevitable as well as good.

Ari   It wasn't that I was looking for a theme. It was that I had always been thinking of those questions of why. "Why?" I'd pinch myself and say that I'm alive. Wait a minute. What does that mean? I look around and I see the world. Oh—where'd it come from? So I was always questioning from the very time I could even think. And I just found out that I kept asking these questions and they seemed to coincide with the idea of how the Universe came into being. And some of the terms that I used in early paintings had long titles that meant the same thing, that were euphemisms. And then finally I got it, I said, "Wait a minute. What are you really asking? You're asking about origin. How did the Universe come into being?" So I thought, "What's the simplest thing that says 'beginning', whether it's the beginning of whatever—just the idea of beginnings."

I think that the other part of the Genesis theme is that I made a commitment to myself to celebrate life. I wasn't going to do the opposite. And that's what my job is, to celebrate life in my work.

Spontaneity is necessary whether you're painting or teaching. My method of spontaneity is to be in the moment. I'm incredibly aware of time. David and I have talked a lot about the different kinds of time—there's time that's chronological that you can very easily describe because it's so late or so early. But there's also the time that is mysterious time, time that is mythic, time that suspends the particular structure of itself. And I'm fascinated by it. I think that's another reason for the Genesis theme because I'm very, very passionate about time, space, matter, and energy.

Time is only a thing we give a name to because we are unable to give it any form. The 'moment' is that one second when you are both in time and space. It can happen when you look at a painting, listen to music, or when you're in love and something wonderful is occurring with another human being. When this happens, time, as we know it, totally disappears, and another kind of existence occurs, which is then over in a split second even though it lasted an eternity. But what happened at that moment?

I've often said that I might be painting for a couple of years, you know on and off and here and there and so forth, and I can remember a moment when something incredible happened—when I disappeared and the painting painted itself. And I stepped back and I said, "Whoa! This is impossible! The violin played itself?" But when that happens in a painting, you realize that that's really what it's all about. All the other stuff is really the banana peel; it's the excess.

David   Kairos is the Greek word for sacred time, and there is no before or after in sacred time. Its every moment is fulfilled. Sometimes, it's translated as "the appointed time" or the "fulfilled time", that is, completed time. Every moment that has ever been, or will ever be, is present in this moment. It's not that when you're in the moment that you've forgotten, or you lose your memory or your capacity for foresight. Past, present, and future are all present in kairos. Before and after, which are concepts relevant to chronological time, chronos time, are not relevant to kairos, sacred time.

Ari   And that's what I'm trying to achieve and what everybody I know who does so-called painting, drawing, sculpture, computer work, whatever—is thirsting for, longing for. And it comes so seldom. There is the organic sexual climax, the spiritual climax, and the esthetic climax—they're the same thing although we give them different names. The spiritual climax is when suddenly you're aware of the Universe. The name that you associate with it depends on what culture and era that you grew up with, but the names all refer to the same thing. We get to that point, to that climax, or that instant, and it's the most precious, incredible experience. And that's why I paint. Hoping to get there again some day. And when I look at a painting or I listen to music or I see an incredible dance, and suddenly I'm aware of this motion, this energy that dance can be—you know, it can be with a person or it can be a bird or it can be a baby's smile. It doesn't make any difference, it's the same dance. That's the Genesis. It's trying to get to that state, no matter what the medium, no matter what the context. Because of the way that I'm wired, painting is my way of getting to that place. But with someone else, it may be through another discipline. And yet, we all get there. This is what is so incredible.

Before going to Cranbrook, I had been at Syracuse, but I learned more by hitchhiking to New York and listening to jazz in the village during the fifties than I did in anything that went on at the school. What I learned from jazz was energy. Music contains the vibration of it being made in the moment. That's really where I learned how to draw —it was through watching real people doing real things. Not only copying them, but feeling what their energy was like. For me, the energy of the music translated itself directly into painting. For someone else, the energy might be translated through words...

David   There are a lot of associated concepts that Ari and I have talked about over the years regarding that concept of Genesis, or creation. Particularly, about the conditions for creativity, because as teachers, we were concerned with that. What kind of circumstances foster creativity? And what kind of circumstances tend to inhibit it?

6

Derek   When Ari and I were working on his presentation to the Art Educators of Minnesota, he said that he believes that creativity is a current that passes through all living things. He was thinking a lot about how to teach, or as the case may be, not teach art, and he said that there is an idea among some art educators that certain students possess an inborn selective talent, or an "art gene". Ari says that it is not the job of the art educator to seek out those individuals who possessed this "art gene", but instead to help all people realize and open up this conduit of creativity that lies within them. Some people come with the valve already open a great deal, and some people don't. But regardless, everyone possesses that current flowing underneath.

Ari   I really feel that all living things are "creative" when they are allowed to be themselves. When a bird is as birdish as a bird could be, it will fly as beautifully as the ambient world will allow. If it tried to be a lion, no matter how wonderful a lion is, it isn't going to fly. So it, in its true birdness, will be everything that it can be. So could a fish, a mountain, a grain of sand, or a Derek! What's interesting is that if we impede that organism from being itself, we are preventing creativity. It's nurturing and liberating to give people permission to be themselves. In creativity, it's the child: if the child is allowed to play, it exhibits the most extraordinary creative behavior. And we as humankind, if we are allowed to play, and I don't mean in a negative sense, but in a positive sense, we can do incredible things. So the question of great music, great poetry, great painting, great whatever, is when people are able to envision it and do it.

The issue of creativity is that if I paint, then I have to allow myself to be myself and not to be Grant Wood. If my model is Grant Wood, and I'm modeling myself after his paintings, then I'm not going to do anything that's very good. I will be a bad Grant Wood. So, I don't model myself after creative people or their work, but I do look at how they do things. And when

I see how they do things, the most important thing is to learn how they make mistakes.

Another reason why I don't like the idea of modeling after someone, is the fact that if I'm in awe of a person, then I don't realize that they are as human as I am and that I am as human as they are. What I've learned is that instead of putting one person or one thing on a pedestal, it has to be a composite. We've got many examples of people doing things and living lives, and it's up to us to assimilate what's good for us. No role model is perfect.

Getting back to what Derek mentioned about the teaching, or non teaching, of art... When a student comes out of high school, the student has already learned how to be a student. In fact, the student learned how to be a student from the time s/he was like one year old. And so the problem is unlearning how to be a student and being able to learn how to live in the moment. I can't remember anything at all of the last 40 years of teaching except the feeling of surprise that comes when you are in the moment and the other person is in the moment, because then something wonderful happens. If you try to design it, to essentially arrange it so that it will occur, it isn't going to happen. If you contrive it, you've lost it. No matter if you're the student, or the teacher, or the parent, or the school—you'll lose it because then it becomes a controlled situation, a power situation. But if you allow it to flow out of the context, out of the moment, out of the spontaneity...

My job as a teacher is not to be there. I'm a mirror, and I'm also a kind of hidden energy source. I've judiciously kept my professional life as an artist separate from my students. If Pam is working with me, then my job is to make Pam the best Pam that there is, and not to have anything of me in it. If I'm working with this person or that person, the idea as a teacher is not to unload what I have upon you.

ARIBERT MUNZNER
TEACHER, COLLEAGUE, ARTIST

Lynn   During all the years that Ari has been my mentor, he's never defined me or my art through the filter of his own experiences. He somehow sees the essence of who I am and what I'm trying to achieve, and masterfully turns the tables so that by the end of each session, I'm telling him what I need to do next.

Ari   When I was at Cranbrook, what I learned from Sepeshy was teaching by metaphor. Sepeshy would come into my studio, look at what I was painting, and then he would tell me a story from when he was a young boy living in Budapest. He didn't talk about the painting. He'd spend a long time describing something in detail, like a Polish wedding that he had attended when he was a child. When he finished the story, he'd walk away, and I knew that the painting needed more red. Teaching by telling stories. That, I felt, was a wonderful way for the mind to be active in terms of the work. You don't say, "Put more green here", instead, it's non-directive teaching.

9

I love teaching by metaphor because then I can avoid trying to be didactic, which I hate to do. Or pedantic. But the other thing that is fun for me to do, is to try, every day, to find a sense of wonder about life and the world. Now, for me, art does this. Music, painting, sculpture, poetry, images, anything in art, an incredible sunset, you know, a fantastic swoop of a bird going, whisk! The sense of wonder means, that at that moment, you really start to wonder. How does one inculcate within oneself, and within others, that sense of wonder? I don't know. All I know is that that's what I'm always searching for and trying to find it in all situations.

A fiddler practices a long time and then comes the concert. And somehow, even though I've heard that song before, wow! That is inspired music. How does one rise from reading the music to inspired music? When we know how to do our craft, whether it is teaching or designing or painting or writing books or whatever, how do you get to that next step where you lose yourself totally and you're into the work?

David   The word "core" comes from the Latin words meaning "heart", and I
see Ari expressing his core essence and his focus wherever he is, whenever
it is. This is a process in which the notion of chaos is central, that is, in the
original Greek sense of that word, which doesn't mean confusion, but
rather, agape. According to ancient Greek mythology, eros, that is, creative
energy, not just sexual energy, is contained in the chaos. This is how mytho-
logically they explain the origin of the world: Genesis. This is how I make
sense of the steam that is everywhere present in Ari's work. Whether it's
black or white or colored, it is something flashing forth out of the core and
focus, out of the energetic chasm or chaos. And that, seems to me, to be a
concept that is relevant to whether you are talking about the Genesis of the
world, cosmogony, or the Genesis of an organism, a living organism, or the
Genesis of a vision or an idea or a thought or an attitude.

Michelle   Your work seems to go from either black and white to vibrant.
Nothing really more subdued.

Ari   I think that the black and white Micro drawings are a key to everything
that I've done over the last 40 years. They really serve as models. If Diderot
tried to depict, with his encyclopedia, all of the knowledge and information
at his time, then the Micro drawings are my little Diderot collection because
they are drawings of the microcosm and the macrocosm. There are twelve
of them, black and white. Over a three year period, I did nothing else but
work on these 12 tiny drawings. I didn't think in terms of that they were
black and white and not color; what I thought about was that I needed to
focus. I would have to meditate to get into a state so I could just be there
and draw. I needed to focus on my whole, to focus on everything that I was
feeling and living with at that time. I had to approach each drawing without
making a blot on it, without suddenly losing my exact frequency, (by frequency, I'm talking about the actual rhythmic frequency), and since I didn't
know what it was, I had to go to each one individually, just like teaching.

I tried to compress within these 2.5" x 2" drawings, references to nature and the universe as well as references to my own feelings. One of the twelve is actually a series of seven galaxies that any astronomer can look at and say, "Oh yes, this is M51, here is this one, here is that one." The rest of them are much more truly mythical kinds of references. In those drawings I have naturalistic images as well as images that might be much more metaphoric in the sense of how they represent feelings and emotions disguised as little critters, disguised as microscopic imagery, disguised as macroscopic imagery. Some of them are quite horrendous, horrible in the sense of bringing fear and bringing confrontation. They might be what Joseph Campbell calls, "the monsters guarding the gate into the journey of life". Others might be much more dimensional in terms of time.

Those Micro drawings also represented the fact that I had to approach each drawing from a completely pure space: I didn't do 50 and then keep the 12 that worked, I did 12 and that was it. They also refer to the question of being with another person, because I can't come and talk with you after having just been confronted by somebody who just slipped on a banana peel. I've got to be able to be with you. I've got to be able to be with that drawing the way that drawing is evolving and not move it towards that drawing which is over there. They represent a kind of discipline that I maintain as part of the artistic process. It's not only the freedom to be able to invent and the freedom to be able to evolve through one's work—it's also the discipline necessary to be able to play the music in such a way that it becomes music instead of sound.

When I was working on the Micro drawings, someone said to me, "You know, you really ought to paint larger. I mean, you're working with Genesis." And then I said, "Oh yeah? Larger than the studio? You mean larger than the city? Larger than the planet? Larger than the galaxy?" But I said to myself, "Okay, so how small can I get?" And I got smaller and smaller and smaller.

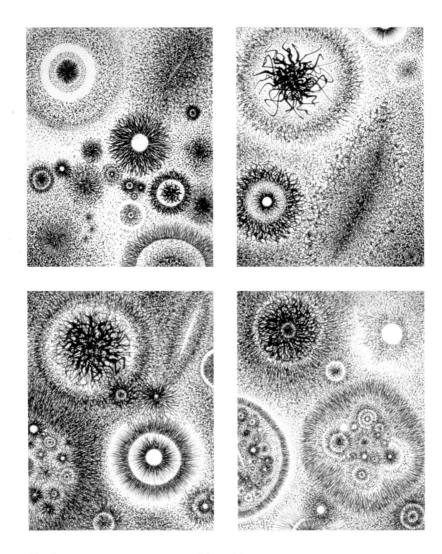

Microdrawings 70-5, 70-6, 70-7, 70-8, 1970. *(left to right)*
2.5" x 2": crow quill pen and India ink on Strathmore paper.
Photos: Rik Sferra, MCAD Professor, Media Arts.

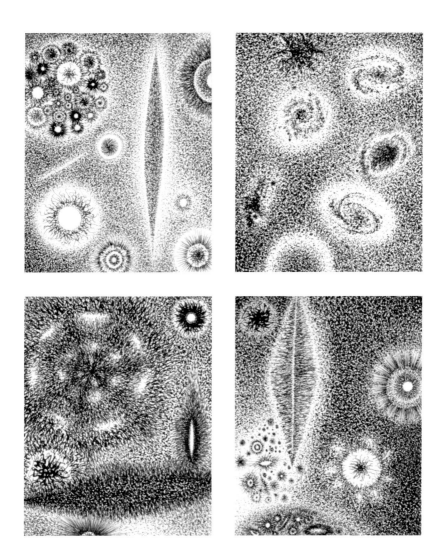

Microdrawings 70-9, 70-10, 71-1, 71-2, 1970-71. *(left to right)*

14

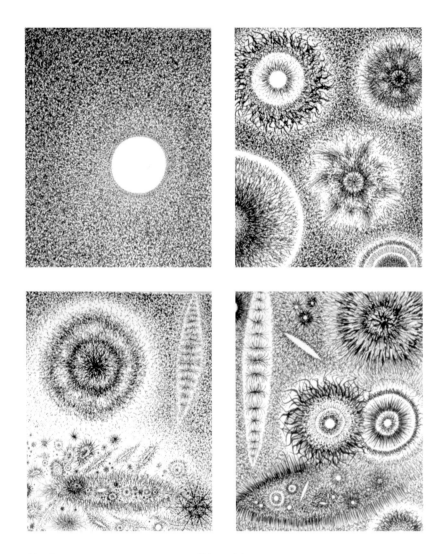

Microdrawings 71-3, 71-4, 71-5, 71-6, 1971. *(left to right)*

David   I think the concept of paradox is crucial to understanding what is going on here. In is out, out is in, far is near, near is far, large is small, small is large.

Ari   So the theme of cosmology is that I look around me, and I never see an object as an object. Yes, it's a cup, but it's made up of atoms; I see the atoms, and they're in motion. It's a table and it's in motion. The room, everything for me is in motion. When I'm in a crowd of people, I see almost spider web-like energies going from person to person. And they spread out continuously throughout the whole planet. So therefore, I cannot localize to draw an object or a person, because whsh! I go right through, you see. I can't stop. So the idea of cosmology is, for me, very exciting, because I go beyond... I go beyond the galaxy, beyond the group of galaxies, or I go so small inside. And therefore, I move between the tiniest and the largest mainly because it moves me into that direction.

Mark   Ari and I spend more time talking about the atmosphere that surrounds the painting than the painting...what are you hearing, what are you smelling. It's not just ,"What are you seeing?" It isn't learning to see with your eyes, but learning how to 'see' internally.

Pam   I have a question that seems sacrilegious in some ways, but I'm curious about it because of your embracing of life and naming your critical work, "Genesis". Do you ever think about death?

Ari   Death? Oh, all the time. That's why I paint. That's the other question, because for me, Genesis is the cycle. The life and death of a star is the same thing. So another star comes. Another galaxy. A little amoeba does its thing. It goes on. And that's so much a part of the cycle that it's been in my work from the very, very beginning. But not in the traditional way of life and death, because I think that's another one of the traps that we get into—is the beginning of life the end of life? And I don't mean any of the religious kind of metaphors. It is so much the whole idea of the life force of the universe being a continuous creation. I'm a tiny part of it, as all of us are a tiny part. The paradox is that we are the part and we are the whole. That's exactly what this is all about.

David   Also, the process of theme and variation that you were describing earlier, is a process of rebirthing. It's not that the painting that becomes finished dies. It has its life. It's been given its life, or it's found its life. And so it's time to move on to another life.

Ari   I was listening to Mahler, and I was aware of Paul Klee's "Angel of Death" in 1944, done just a few months before he died. He put everything into that painting. So, as I was listening to Mahler—this was his last symphony— I remembered that Mahler was similarly being aware of moments that were precious. So I doodled this right on the program during the symphony. And I started down here, and I was listening to in-between the notes, and then I did this up here, and I was thinking, "What's going to happen? What's the relationship between life as we know it, and then when we disappear, our legacy and all that?" I was interested in the transition, the transition that is going on all the time. Someone who is very adept, like a yogi, is able to live in the transition and move in and out of consciousness with perfect ease. Later, I did a drawing from that Mahler program. I got about 20 or 30 more drawings from that, and I'm still working on them.

And then came this painting, last month. In conversations with David, I discovered that what I did was very simply: eliminate this, eliminate that, and work only with the transition. So I'm very intrigued by this idea of transition. This is how the evolution takes place. So you ask, "Do I think about death?" I tell you: every day. All the time. But at the same time, I'm also thinking about the life force.

Ari in his studio on Bryant Avenue, 1978. Photo: John Kruth, MCAD B.F.A., 1979.

Genesis, 1956 #1, 1956.
48" x 36": dry pigment and polymer tempera on masonite.
Collection of Rabbi and Mrs. Meyer Eisemann, Netanya, Israel.

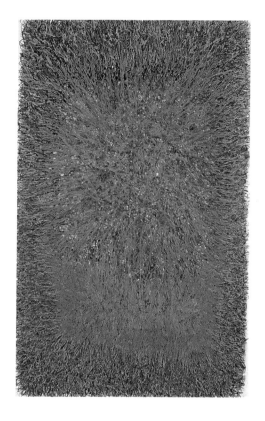

Genesis, February 1963, 1963.
38" x 23": casein on rice paper.
Collection of Joan Munzner.

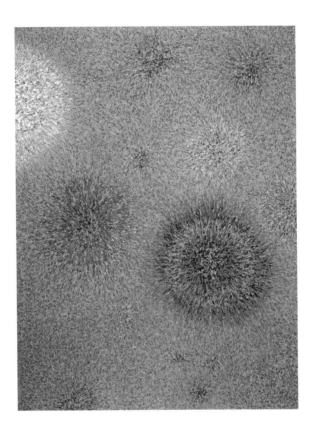

Genesis, Summer 1965 #9, 1965.
20" x 16": casein & vinyl on plexiglas.
Collection of Dolly Fiterman.
Photo: A. Kenneth Olson.

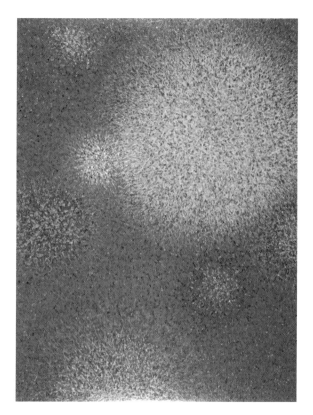

Genesis, 1968 #6, 1968.
20" x 16": casein & vinyl on plexiglas.
Collection of Joan Munzner.

(Right) Ari standing in front of Genesis, 1968 #6, 3M Scanamural, 1976. 96" x 68": acrylic on canvas. Photo· John T. Sherman.

Genesis, 80-1, 1980.
20" x 16", casein and vinyl on plexiglas.
Collection of the estate of A. Kenneth Olson.
Photo: A. Kenneth Olson.

Genesis, 83-1, 1983.
20" x 16", casein and vinyl on plexiglas.
Collection of Joan Munzner.
Photo: A. Kenneth Olson.

Genesis, 82-R9, 1982.
39" x 25": casein on rice paper.
Collection of Joan Munzner.
Photo: A. Kenneth Olson.

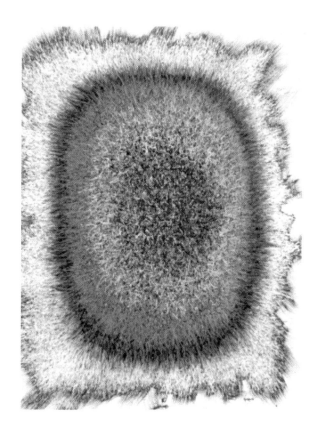

Genesis 3/31/96, 1996.
26" x 20": casein on paper board.

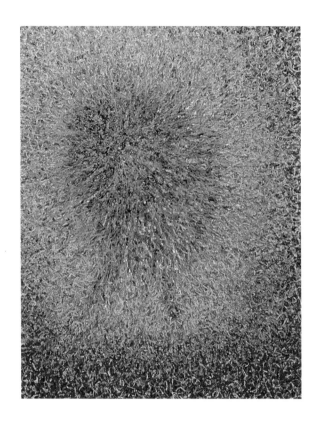

Genesis 94-1, 1994.
60" x 48": acrylic on canvas.
Collection of Dolly Fiterman.

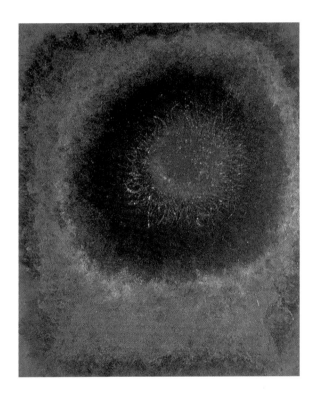

Genesis 97-6, 1997.
40" x 32": acrylic on board.
Photo: Alex Steinberg, MCAD B.F.A., 1998.

Genesis 3/20/96, 1996.
10" x 8": color pencil on black paper board.
Collection of Rabbi and Mrs. Leon Olenick, Miami, Florida.

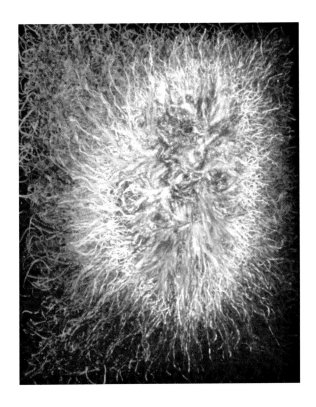

Genesis 3/24/96, 1996.
10" x 8": color pencil on black paper board.
Collection of Marian Eisner and Rich Kessler.

Genesis 98-4, 1998.
36" x 24": acrylic on canvas.
Photo: Alex Steinberg.

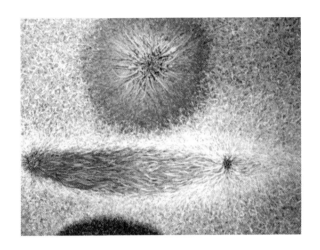

Genesis, 98-6, 1998.
36" x 48": acrylic on canvas.
Photo: Alex Steinberg.

32

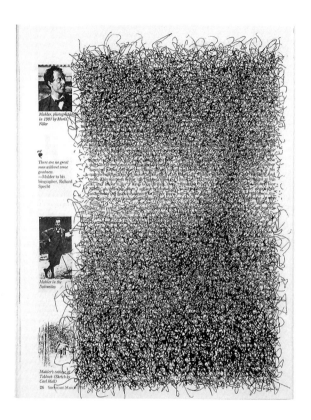

Genesis (Mahler's Ninth), 1992.
10.5" x 7.5": pen and ink on concert program.
Collection of Marian Eisner and Rich Kessler.
Photo: Alex Steinberg.

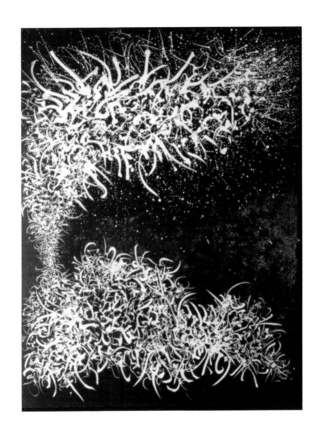

Genesis 5-22-98, 1998.
48" x 36": acrylic on canvas.
Photo: Alex Steinberg.

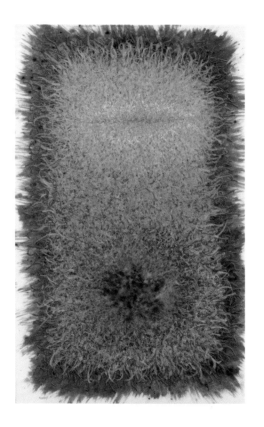

Genesis 98-3(R), 1998.
39" x 24": acrylic on rice paper.
Collection of Joan Munzner.

Genesis 98-13, 1998.
10" x 8": acrylic on canvas.
Collection of Lynn Golberstein.

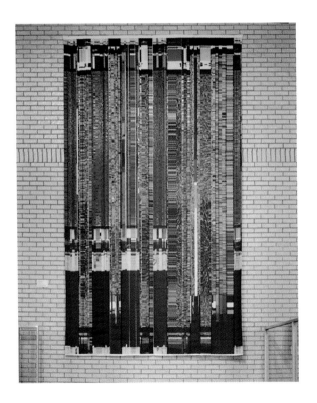

Genesis, 82-1,1982.
3M Scanamural Color Experiment.
160" x 100": acrylic on canvas.
MCAD Gallery Installation, Photo: Rik Sferra.

(right) 3M Scanamural System ad.

The Painting Computer

Genesis, 82-3 and Genesis 82-1, 1982.
3M Scanamural Color Experiments, MCAD Gallery Installation.

(Right) Exhibition Card, Dolly Fiterman Gallery, 1984.
Photo: Mark Norberg.

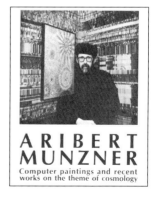

A R I B E R T
MUNZNER
Computer paintings and recent
works on the theme of cosmology

Genesis 84-4, 1984.
3M BFA Computer Paint System.
35mm Ektachrome Transparency: A. Kenneth Olson.

Ari Munzner, in his studio at the 3M BFA Computer Paint System, 1998.
Photo: Sean Smuda, *City Pages*.

Genesis, Micro/Macro #3, 1986.
3M BFA Computer Paint System.
35mm Ektachrome Transparency: A. Kenneth Olson.

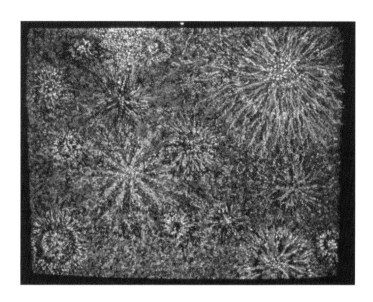

Genesis, Micro/Macro #2, 1986.
3M BFA Computer Paint System.
35mm Ektachrome Transparency: A. Kenneth Olson.

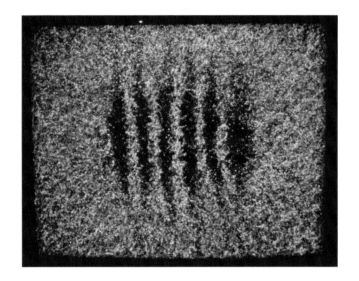

Genesis, Micro/Macro #18 1986, 1986.
3M BFA Computer Paint System.
35mm Ektachrome Transparency: A. Kenneth Olson.

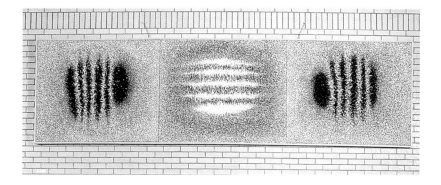

Genesis, Triptych 1988, 1988.
48" x 180": acrylic on canvas.
MCAD Gallery Installation.
Photo: Rik Sferra.

Dolly Fiterman and Ari standing before *Genesis 98-4*,
at the opening of *"Works on Cosmology"*, Dolly Fiterman Fine Arts, 1999.
Photos: Klaus Henning Hansen.

ARIBERT MUNZNER, A SENSE OF WONDER

Introduction by Dolly Fiterman

Aribert Munzner was the first artist I presented when I opened my Gallery in 1976 and, since then, his work has been exhibited at Dolly Fiterman Fine Arts in individual and group exhibitions. He has exhibited widely both in the region and nationally, and his work is included in many museum, corporate and private collections nationwide.

In a time of unprecedented scientific revelations and pioneering space explorations, our culture has been confronted by questions of our place in the universe. For many decades Aribert has been working on his Genesis series, synthesizing the areas of art, science and mythology. His paintings address the relationship of the microcosm to the macrocosm through complex calligraphic brush strokes that create fields of color energy. These glowing abstractions reveal a process of becoming, or blooming, like flowers or expanding like new universes. Subtle color gradations and delicate shifts in hue produce a dense and richly textured surface, active and alive like microscopic organisms or cosmic shimmering voids.

The underlying rhythms of his brushstrokes reveal an intuitive musical dance that changes with each work to conform to the scale, proportion and concept of the vision unfolding. The musical nature of the paintings are another manifestation of his search for an art which reveals the energies, movements, vibrations, frequencies and transformations of nature from the primordial to the infinite.

Aribert is a totally dedicated painter and a true visionary in that he has laid the foundation for future generations. I see him as an artist who stimulates a sense of belonging to the universe by creating unique experiences through cosmic imagery.

Dolly Fiterman, *Director and CEO Dolly Fiterman Fine Arts*
August 12th, 1999

To The McKnight Foundation:

' "I write in support of the nomination of MCAD Professor Emeritus Aribert Munzner for the McKnight Distinguished Artist Award.

Ari Munzner's art career spans many years and offers accomplishments of excellence in so many different sectors of the visual arts.

As a painter and student of color, Ari has evolved a special vision of retinal/spiritual symbolism. His vibrant studies challenge the viewer in both sensory and religious sensibilities.

As a teacher, he has devoted the years of his career to the expressive enablement and intellectual illumination of his students. They have shown great loyalty to this devotion of service and honor him in their recollections to us and their personal creative accomplishments.

Ari has spoken far and wide in the community and the state. He has represented the vigor of creative thinking to national audiences in the fields of education and art.

Ari has developed a magnificent network of friends and supporters. They are lovingly and respectfully a heritage for this community of his own careful making.

Certainly, he is one of our most distinguished artists; his art, his citizenship and his creativity have provided a vision and example for well over four decades. He is well known to so many and yet little known as well. His contributions have been so very large; his formal exhibition achievements gave way throughout his mature life to unselfish contributions to the lives of hundreds of artists of the region!" '

Sincerely,

John S. Slorp, *President, Minneapolis College of Art and Design*
February 24, 1998

' "This book is to honor the work of artist Aribert Munzner, thirty-eight year veteran of the faculty at Minneapolis College of Art and Design and continuing inspiritor as beloved Professor Emeritus since 1994.

Ari profoundly influenced the evolution of the College as an artist, teacher and administrator. With this publication we hope to preserve and share at least a small portion of his philosophy and his art.

Thanks to Ari for allowing us to document the dialogue that forms the text of this book; to Lynn Golberstein whose idea it was to honor Ari in this way; to Pam Arnold for her beautiful design of this book; to Michelle Ollie whose job it was to get this publication produced; and to MCAD President John Slorp who enthusiastically approved and supported the project." '

Andrea Nasset, *Vice President and Dean of Academic Affairs*
Minneapolis College of Art and Design
January, 2000

The following are excerpted from letters written
to the McKnight Distinguished Artist Awards Committee

' "When Ari is present with one, he is entirely present, this is the only way he knows to be. As he gives prodigiously, so he works prodigiously. A visit into his world, the world of his paintings and studio, is a visit into the world of the cosmos, for Ari is able to find the cosmos in the finest, microscopic detail. Under his scrutiny, the part becomes the whole. He brings love, focus, adventure and discovery to all that he touches, and he has touched much and many." '

Franciska Rosenthal Louw, *MCAD B.F.A., 1991*
March 5th, 1998

' "As a teacher, mentor, and advisor to undergraduate and graduate students, Ari is stellar - a teacher's teacher. As an administrator, Ari wore practically every hat there is at MCAD. As an artist in the world he is prolific and respected.

However, I would say, what I appreciate most about Ari is a fundamental enthusiasm that permeates every activity in which he participates. Agree with him in point or not, there is no doubt that he is present. He exudes an energy, a curiosity and a love of life that is unparalleled. It is an honor for me to be his colleague and friend." '

> Judith Sarah Rae, *Executive Assistant to the Academic Dean*
> *Minneapolis College of Art and Design*
> February 28th, 1998

' "I have known Ari and his work for over thirty years. I regard him as one of the most distinguished artists. He is one of the few artists who combines science, art perception and visual imagination" '

> Robert Suderburg, *Composer in Residence, Professor of Music, Williams College*
> March 16th, 1998

' "He is an example of the enduring value of personal voice in the Arts. Maestro Munzner stands as a beacon and mentor to many of my generation. There is no other artist I know of who has offered such a profound example of pure pursuit in the arts. Aribert has been my 'Art Father' throughout my life in the Arts." '

> Aldo L. Moroni, *Artist*
> March 1st, 1998

' "Aribert constantly amazes me with his enthusiasm for life and art; he has vitality that is contagious…there is something so glorious about this beatnik, whose computer art, his performative talks, his way of life, all add up to make him one of the most distinctive people I know. He is an incredible role model." '

Karen Wirth, *Chair, Foundation/Fine Arts*
College of Visual Arts, Saint Paul, Minnesota
March 15th, 1998

' "Professor and Dean Emeritus, Aribert Munzner…probes the boundaries of discovery whether exploring his own place in the world through a mythic cosmology of painting, drawing and new technologies, or working intently with young artists. He is a genuine leader, quickly effecting change through others. He is the quintessential artist role model for the creative decision maker of the twenty-first century.

His work as an artist is that of the dance. His strokes move quickly across the canvas in dazzling virtuosity. Whirling in brilliant color, line becomes mass becomes subject becomes the known becomes the unknowable. His is a constant search for depth. His work professes an awe for the spiritual and a consistent optimism." '

Ellen L. Meyer, *President, The Atlanta College of Art*
March 27th, 1998

' "The pictures Aribert has painted with painstaking detail make me enter into a visionary tunnel in which I sense that I am present at the emerging moments of life. The vision of the bio-genesis of cells and plants, of bourgeoning bacterial and animal life forms stimulates my meditation and draws me ever deeper into the process where we all began. This is the genius of his inner contemplation made into graphic form that allows another to enter into the imaginal work he creates. " '

Rabbi Zalman M. Schlachter-Shalomi, M.A., D.H.L.
World Wisdom Chair – Naropa Institute
Professor Emeritus of Religion, Temple University
March 15th, 1998

50

' "In talking to Ari one is reminded –I use the word in its literal sense: re-minded, brought back to mindfulness– of essential things: the joyfulness of inner child, the inevitable experience of pain, the resources of creativity. I know from observation and anecdote that his instinct for the essential and his timing are finely tuned. I have seen the evidence in the way he works with younger artists, and in his paintings , in passages from closed to open gesture, from stillness to breath. What Ari has built are not enormous monuments, but deep fertilizations of the spirit, encouraging a reverence for what might be possible. We are significantly richer for his company." '

Joyce Lyon, *Artist, Associate Professor, University of Minnesota*
March 13th, 1998